GCSE Mathematics

Foundation Level
Revision With Exam Practice (For the New Grade 9 - 1 Exams)

HOW TO PASS MY GCSE MATHS IN 4 WEEKS

WEEK 1 DAY 1 - Number

Many students think GCSE Maths is tough and to get a passing grade is tougher than ever. Even in the Foundation Level, many failed to get the passing grade they needed. This is NOT how it is suppose to be.

So this is where we have taken all the important topics and facts and separated them into easy to learn and remember daily workloads. There are 28 days of workloads, hence 28 booklets. By reading and understanding the notes given in each booklet, you will get the knowledge, experience and foundation in Maths that you need to pass your GCSE Maths Foundation Level. Then there are simple exercises to get you started. When you are ready, move on to the actual GCSE past exam questions and fully worked answers. Finally, print out the exam past questions and give it a go yourself. When you can get all questions correct from all the booklets, then you are ready and prepared for your GCSE Maths Foundation Level exam.

These 4 weeks - 28 days booklets are a crash course and easy to follow exercises to assist you to get the passing grade that you need in the Foundation Level.

- All the questions from the previous Exam Papers New Grade 1-9
  Year 2017 and 2018
- Extensive coverage of Grade 9-1 GCSE Maths course
  including topics that you need to know to answer all exam questions
- Answers included
  including workings for those difficult exam questions

How to Use This Booklet

- Mark your calendar to do each booklet a day for 28 days in 4 weeks before your exam. Or if you are preparing ahead of time before your GCSE, do one booklet per week for 7 months.
- Study and remember everything in the Revision section of this booklet.
- Work on the exercises.
- Study the Practice Exam Questions examples and workings. Understand the question, reasoning, the logic and workings and solutions for each question.
- Print the Practice Exam Questions section (without answers) and attempt to answer them correctly.
- Repeat the past exam questions until you get them all correct and you feel confident about the topics discussed on this booklet.
- Repeat the revision if necessary before any tests or exam.
- Attempt other past papers when you have done all the 28 days booklets.

Revision

Type of Numbers

Integers - An integer is a whole number. Either a positive or negative number, or zero.

Examples

Integers: -35, -7, 0, 1, 2, 19, 189, 1 923 500

Non Integers: -1.002, 0.5, $\frac{3}{4}$, $\sqrt{6}$, 33.333,

Decimals numbers are based on 10 digits (0,1,2,3,4,5,6,7,8 and 9). Decimal number is often used to mean a number that uses a **decimal point** followed by digits that show a value smaller than one. Example

 45.2 (forty-five **point** two)

Rational numbers can be written as fractions. Most numbers you deal with are rational. Rational numbers come in 3 different forms:

1. Integers - 4 (= $\frac{4}{1}$)
2. Fractions ($\frac{p}{q}$) where p and q are non-zero integers -$\frac{1}{4}$
3. Terminating or recurring decimals - 0.125, 0.133333...., 0.143143143

Irrational numbers are messy numbers. They can't be written as fractions, meaning they are never ending, non-repeating decimals.

Square root ($\sqrt{x}$) of positive integers are either integers or irrational numbers

Example

$\sqrt{2}$ is irrational

$\sqrt{4}$ is 2 (integer, rational)

BODMAS

Brackets, Other, Division, Multiplication, Addition, Subtraction

When performing a calculation, **BODMAS** tell you the **order** in which the operations should be done. Work out the **Brackets** first, then **Other** things like **squares** and **indices**, then **Divide** and/or **Multiply** groups of numbers before **Adding** and/or **Subtracting** them.

Example

Solve $\sqrt{4 + 6 \times (12 - 2)}$

$$\sqrt{4 + 6 \times (12 - 2)} = \sqrt{4 + 6 \times (10)}$$
$$= \sqrt{4 + 60}$$
$$= \sqrt{64}$$
$$= 8$$

Base 10 Numbers

The numbers we use in our daily life and is commonly use around the world is called Base 10 Numbers. Base 10 refers to the numbering system which uses 10 digits. Each digit in a position of a number can have an integer value ranging from 0 to 9. The 10 digits are 0, 1, 2, 3, 4, 5, 6, 7, 8 and 9 and we have 10 possibilities. Also, the numbering systems allow decimals numbers for fractions of a whole unit.

Starting from 0, 1, 2, 3, 4, 5, 6, 7, 8, 9, we have used up all single digit.

Next, we move to 2 digits starting from 10, 11, 12, 13, 14, 15, 16, 17, 18, 19. See how 1st position uses 1 and 2nd position is from 0 to 9.

Then we move on to 2 on the 1st position and restart 0 to 9 again. This makes 20, 21, 22, 23, 24, 25, 26, 27, 28, 29

Now you can see the pattern for 2 digits. When we hit the final 2 digits 99, we need 3 digits.

So now you can see we have units (1 digit), tenths (2 digits), hundredths (3 digits), thousands (4 digits), ten thousandths (5 digits), hundred thousandths (6 digits), millionths (7 digits) and the number gets bigger.

Decimals starts when we have a fraction of 1 unit. So instead of writing in fraction format, we can write the portions of the unit in decimals using a '.' (decimal point). So anything after the decimal point is smaller than 1.

0.1 - this is $\frac{1}{10}$

0.01 - this is $\frac{1}{100}$

0.001 - this is $\frac{1}{1000}$

So you can see how we can use Base 10 numbers to make a number really big using many digits and positions or really small using decimal point and many digits and position after the decimal point.

Multiplication

You must know how to multiply by hand without a calculator. Practise, practise, practice.

Whole numbers

245×54

Working:

1) Align all the units of both numbers below each other.

2) Then multiply the 1st number with the unit of the 2nd row

3) Then multiply the 1st number with the tenths of the 2nd row and move the answer to tenth position and fill in 0 in the space. Repeat when there are move positions in the 2nd number.

4) Finally, when all multiplication is done, add up all the numbers.

```
        2 4 5

  x       5 4

    _____

        9 8 0

    1 2 2 5 0

  +_____

    1 3 2 3 0

    =========
```

Decimals

24.5×0.54

Working:

1) When multiplying decimals, ignore the decimal places of both numbers to begin with and just perform as if both numbers are whole numbers multiplication.

2) After completed the whole numbers multiplication, count how many decimal places from both numbers and put the decimal point back to this position on your final answer.

```
        2 4 5

  x       5 4

  _____

        9 8 0

    1 2 2 5 0

  +_____

    1 3 . 2 3 0

  =========
```
(1 decimal place in 1st number and 2 decimal places in 2nd number, hence 3dp.)

Division

You must know how to divide by hand without a calculator. Practise, practise, practice.

Whole numbers

$376 \div 8$

Working:

1) Read the question - "376 divide by 8". So 376 goes inside, divide by 8 goes outside.

2) Take the first number, see if there is a number that times 8 goes into 3. If not, put a 0 as the answer on top of 3, then carry down 3 and bring the next number down making it 37.

```
        0
     _____
  8 ) 3 7 6

     3 7
```

3) What number times 8 goes into 37? The answer is 4 because 4 x 8 = 32. Put 4 on top of 7 now. 4 x 8 = 32, so put 32 under 37. Subtract and take the remainder into next line and bring down the next number making it 56.

```
    0  4
8 ) 3  7  6
    3  7
  - 3  2
      5  6
```

4) What number times 8 goes into 56? The answer is 7. Put 7 on top of 6 now. 7 x 8 = 56, so put 56 under 56 from the previous step. Subtract and no remainder. Done.

```
    0  4  7
8 ) 3  7  6
    3  7
  - 3  2
      5  6
    - 5  6
         0
```

5) The answer is on top of the division working, which is 47.

Decimals

37.6 ÷ 0.08

When dividing a decimal number, it is easier to make the number whole before starting the division. In this example, we would not divide by 0.08, but instead divide by 8. So to make 0.8 to become 8, we have to multiply by 100 (multiply by 100 moves the decimal point 2 places to the right, making the number bigger by 100th). And by multiplying the 0.8 by 100, we have to multiply everything else by 100. So 37.6 becomes 3760.

Now start the normal division for 3760 ÷ 8 = 470

```
       0  4  7  0
8 ) 3  7  6  0
    3  7
  - 3  2
       5  6
     - 5  6
          0  0
```

Multiples

The multiples of a number are just the times table.

Example

The multiples of 8 is 8, 16, 24, 32, 40, 48, 56, 64, 2, 80, 88, 96, ...

Factor

The factors of a number are any numbers that divide into it exactly. Remember that factors always comes in pairs because 2 x 4 is the same as 4 x 2. Sometimes it is easier to draw a big loop and put the pair of factors across each other. Then at the bottom of the loop is the final pair of factors because no other numbers in between this pair are factors of that number.

Example

The factors of 24 are 1, 2, 3, 4, 6, 8, 12, 24.

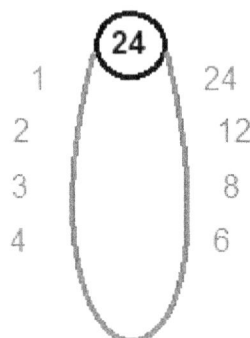

Prime Factors

A prime number has exactly two factors (1 and number itself). It doesn't divide by any other numbers apart from itself and 1. Note 1 is NOT a prime number.

The prime numbers are 2, 3, 5, 7, 11, 13, 17, 19, 23, 29, 31, 37, 41, 43, ...

If a number is a factor of another number and it is a prime number, then it is called a prime factor. You can use a factor tree to find prime factors. Remember to circle the prime numbers in the tree so that you know that is the last number in the branch and cannot be divided into other numbers.

Example

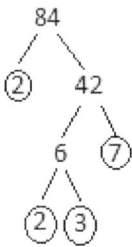

Hence, $84 = 2 \times 2 \times 3 \times 7$ (all prime numbers)

$= 2^2 \times 3 \times 7$ (product of its prime factor in index form)

HCF (Highest Common Factor)
HCF is the biggest number that will DIVIDE INTO ALL the numbers.

To find the HCF, circle all the prime numbers which are common to both products of prime factors. Then multiply the circled numbers together to find the HCF.

Examples

Work out the HCF of 108 and 24. (Find the biggest number that will divide into 108 and 24.)

24 $\quad = 2 \times 2 \times 2 \times 3$

108 $\quad = 2 \times 2 \times 3 \times 3 \times 3$

HCF is $2 \times 2 \times 3 = 2^2 \times 3 = 12$

LCM (Lowest Common Multiple)
LCM is the smallest number that will DIVIDE BY ALL the numbers.

To find the LCM, multiply the HCF by the numbers in both products that were not circled in the HCF. Or select the highest index for each unique prime factors.

Work out the LCM of 108 and 24. (Find the smallest number that can be divided by 108 and 24.)

24 $\quad = 2 \times 2 \times 2 \times 3$

108 $\quad = 2 \times 2 \times 3 \times 3 \times 3$

LCM is $12 \times 2 \times 3 \times 3 = 216$

or

LCM is $2 \times 2 \times 2 \times 3 \times 3 \times 3 = 2^3 \times 3^3 = 216$

Extra Notes

Multiples of 24 is   24, 48, 72, 96, 120, 144, 168, 192, **216**, 140

Multiples of 108 is   108, **216**, 324

Lowest common multiples (LCM) of 24 and 108 is **216**.

Practice Exam Questions Examples

2017 June P1 ✗	2 (1) marks	Write 7.26451 correct to 3 decimal places. 7·265| ⌣⌣⌣
2017 June P1 ✗	22 (2)	Express 56 as the product of its prime factors. 56 ② 28 ② 14 ② ⑦ 2×2×2×7
2017 June P1 ✗	23 (3)	Work out 54.6 × 4.3 5 4 6 × 4 3 1 6 3 8 + 2 1 8 4 0 2 3 4·7 8
2017 June P2	8a (1)	Here is a list of numbers. 21 22 23 24 25 26 27 28 29 From the numbers in the list, write down a square number. 25 (5×5)
2017 June P2	8b (1)	From the numbers in the list, write down a number that is a multiple of **both** 4 and 6 24 (4×6)
2017 June	8c	Write down all the prime numbers in the list.

P2	(1)	23 , 29
2017 June P2	(2)	Find the value of $$\frac{\sqrt{13.4 - 1.5}}{(6.8 + 0.06)^2}$$ Write down all the figures on your calculator display. 0.07330359081
2017 June P3	1a (1)	The table shows the lengths of five rivers. <table><tr><th>River</th><th>Length (km)</th></tr><tr><td>Trent</td><td>297</td></tr><tr><td>Don</td><td>112</td></tr><tr><td>Severn</td><td>354</td></tr><tr><td>Thames</td><td>346</td></tr><tr><td>Mersey</td><td>113</td></tr></table> Write down the rivers in order of length. Start with the shortest river. Don, Mersey, Trent, Thames, Severn
	1b (1)	Ami says, "The River Thames is more than three times as long as the River Don." Show that Ami is correct. $\begin{array}{r}112\\ \times\ \ 3\\ \hline 336\end{array}$ Thames 346 > 336
2017 June P3	3 (2)	Here are four digits. 5 6 1 9 (i) Write down the smallest possible two digit number that can be made with two of the digits. 15 (ii) Write down the three digit number closest to 200 that can be made with three of the digits.

		196
2017 June P3	8 (2)	Joanne wants to buy a dishwasher. The dishwasher costs £372 Joanne will pay a deposit of £36 She will then pay the rest of the cost in 4 equal monthly payments. How much is each monthly payment? $$£\ 3\overset{6}{\cancel{7}}2$$ $$-\ \ 36$$ $$£336$$ $$£84$$ $$4)\overline{336}$$ $$-32\,6$$ $$16$$ £84 monthly payment
2018 June P1	1 (1)	Write 6324 correct to the nearest thousand. 6000
2018 June P1	2a (1)	Write the following numbers in order of size. Start with the smallest number. -6 6 -5 0 12 -6, -5, 0, 6, 12
	2b (1)	Write the following numbers in order of size. Start with the smallest number. 0.078 0.78 0.87 0.708 0.078, 0.708, 0.78, 0.87
2018 June P1	5 (1)	Write down the first even multiple of 7 14
2018 June P1	11a (1)	Write down an example to show that each of the following two statements is not correct. The factors of an even number are always even. 3 x 4 = 12
	11b	All the digits in odd numbers are odd. 23

	(1)	
2018 June P2	4 (1)	Write down a 6 digit number that has 4 as its thousands digit. You can only use the digit 4 once. 12 4,158
2018 June P2	6 (3)	Margaret is thinking of a number. She says, "My number is odd. It is a factor of 36 and a multiple of 3" There are two possible numbers Margaret can be thinking of. Write down these two numbers. 36 ③ ⑨ 3, 9
2018 June P2	10a (2)	Write down all the prime numbers between 20 and 30 23 , 29
	10b (1)	Catherine says, "2 is the only even prime number." Is Catherine right? You must give a reason for your answer. Yes, all even numbers greater than 2 has a factor of 2.
2018 June P2	21a (2)	Find the lowest common multiple (LCM) of 40 and 56 56 40 ② 28 ② 20 ② 14 ② 10 ② ⑦ ② ⑤ $2^3 \times 7$ $2^3 \times 5$ $LCM = 2^3 \times 5 \times 7$ $= 280$
	21a (1)	$A = 2^3 \times 3 \times 5$ $B = 2^2 \times 3 \times 5^2$ Write down the highest common factor (HCF) of A and B $HCF = 2^2 \times 3 \times 5$ $= 60$
2018	5a	Here are four digits.

June P3	(1)	7 3 4 9 Use three of these digits to write down the largest possible 3-digit number. 974
	5b (1)	Here are four different digits. 8 2 1 6 Put one of these digits in each box to give the smallest possible answer to the sum. You must use each digit only once. ☐☐ + ☐☐ 1 8 and 2 6
2018 June P3	6 (2)	Write down all the factors of 30 30 1 — 30 2 — 15 3 — 10 5 — 6 1, 2, 3, 5, 6, 10, 15, 30
2018 June P3	7 (2)	David has twice as many cousins as Becky. Becky has twice as many cousins as Nishat. Nishat has 6 cousins. How many cousins does David have? Becky — 6×2 = 12 David — 12×2 = 24 cousins.
2018 June P3	15a (1)	Jenny is asked to find the value of $12 - 2 \times 4$ Here is her working. $$12 - 2 \times 4 = 10 \times 4 = 40$$ Jenny's answer is wrong. Explain what Jenny has done wrong. Multiplication must be done first, then subtraction. $12 - 2 \times 4 = 12 - 8 = 4$
	15b	Rehan is asked to find the range of the numbers 3 1 8 7 5

(1)

Here is his working.

Range $= 5 - 3 = 2$

This is wrong.
Explain why.

Range is largest - smallest

$8 - 1 = 7$

Practice Exam Questions

Now, rework these exam questions without referring to the notes or answers. Then check your answers and workings against the Examples section. Make sure you get them 100% right and that you understand the topics discussed, not just merely memorizing these questions and answers. Note that there are sometimes multiple ways to find a solution. It doesn't matter. Just stick to the ones that you are most comfortable with and make sense to you.

2017 June P1	2 (1) marks	Write 7.26451 correct to 3 decimal places.
2017 June P1	22 (2)	Express 56 as the product of its prime factors.
2017 June P1	23 (3)	Work out 54.6×4.3
2017 June P2	8a (1)	Here is a list of numbers. 21 22 23 24 25 26 27 28 29 From the numbers in the list, write down a square number.
2017 June P2	8b (1)	From the numbers in the list, write down a number that is a multiple of **both** 4 and 6
2017 June P2	8c (1)	Write down all the prime numbers in the list.
2017 June P2	12 (2)	Find the value of $\dfrac{\sqrt{13.4-1.5}}{(6.8+0.06)^2}$ Write down all the figures on your calculator display.

2017 June P3	1a (1)	The table shows the lengths of five rivers. 	River	Length (km)	 	Trent	297	 	Don	112	 	Severn	354	 	Thames	346	 	Mersey	113	 Write down the rivers in order of length. Start with the shortest river.
	1b (1)	Ami says, "The River Thames is more than three times as long as the River Don." Show that Ami is correct.
2017 June P3	3 (2)	Here are four digits. 5 6 1 9 (i) Write down the smallest possible two digit number that can be made with two of the digits. (ii) Write down the three digit number closest to 200 that can be made with three of the digits.
2017 June P3	8 (2)	Joanne wants to buy a dishwasher. The dishwasher costs £372 Joanne will pay a deposit of £36 She will then pay the rest of the cost in 4 equal monthly payments. How much is each monthly payment?

2018 June P1	1 (1)	Write 6324 correct to the nearest thousand.
2018 June P1	2a (1)	Write the following numbers in order of size. Start with the smallest number. -6 6 -5 0 12
	2b (1)	Write the following numbers in order of size. Start with the smallest number. 0.078 0.78 0.87 0.708
2018 June P1	5 (1)	Write down the first even multiple of 7
2018 June P1	11a (1)	Write down an example to show that each of the following two statements is not correct. The factors of an even number are always even.
	11b (1)	All the digits in odd numbers are odd.
2018 June P2	4 (1)	Write down a 6 digit number that has 4 as its thousands digit. You can only use the digit 4 once.

2018 June P2	6 (3)	Margaret is thinking of a number. She says, "My number is odd. It is a factor of 36 and a multiple of 3" There are two possible numbers Margaret can be thinking of. Write down these two numbers.
2018 June P2	10a (2)	Write down all the prime numbers between 20 and 30
	10b (1)	Catherine says, "2 is the only even prime number." Is Catherine right? You must give a reason for your answer.
2018 June P2	21a (2)	Find the lowest common multiple (LCM) of 40 and 56
	21a (1)	$A = 2^3 \times 3 \times 5 \qquad\qquad B = 2^2 \times 3 \times 5^2$ Write down the highest common factor (HCF) of A and B
2018 June P3	5a (1)	Here are four digits. 7 3 4 9 Use three of these digits to write down the largest possible 3-digit number.

	5b (1)	Here are four different digits. <div align="center">8 2 1 6</div>Put one of these digits in each box to give the smallest possible answer to the sum. You must use each digit only once. <div align="center">◻◻ + ◻◻</div>
2018 June P3	6 (2)	Write down all the factors of 30
2018 June P3	7 (2)	David has twice as many cousins as Becky. Becky has twice as many cousins as Nishat. Nishat has 6 cousins. How many cousins does David have?
2018 June P3	15a (1)	Jenny is asked to find the value of $12 - 2 \times 4$ Here is her working. $12 - 2 \times 4 = 10 \times 4 = 40$ Jenny's answer is wrong. Explain what Jenny has done wrong.

	15b	Rehan is asked to find the range of the numbers
		3 1 8 7 5
	(1)	Here is his working.
		Range $= 5 - 3 = 2$
		This is wrong.
		Explain why.

ADVICE

To pass your GCSE maths papers isn't just about working on past papers but your ability to apply everything that you have learnt and all the formulas that you must remember to answer and solve all the questions. Then practise, practise, practise. Then check your progress using past papers and time yourself. Ensure you can complete all the questions within the time allowed plus 15 minutes to double check all your answers for all the questions. If you get most of the questions correct, then you know you have done well.

For the non-calculator paper, make sure you learn and remember your **times table**.

Guidelines:

- Read the question carefully and understand the question. Mentally note down all the information that is given to you.
- Look at the marks given for each question. This usually is a good indicator how many steps or workings you need to give to get full mark on the question. Usually 1 mark for each step of workings and 1 mark for the answer.
- Check out command words carefully to understand what the question is asking of you.
- Use past papers to make sure that you are managing your time well.
- Set yourself a time frame to complete each question. If you spend more than 5 minutes on 1 question, move on to another question and come back to this at the end of the paper.
- Go through past paper answers, highlight any marks you lose or mistakes you make.
- Test yourself. Find out if your revision has been effective by using past papers or ask someone to test you.
- If your notes are all bullet points, past papers might be the first chance you have to write in clear and linked sentences.
- Repeat your tests – it is important you test yourself more than once. Try it ten minutes after revising a topic, one day after, then a week later. Then a month later.

Command words and their definitions

Describe	say what you see - no need for reasons
Explain	give reasons
Outline	give a brief summary
Analyse	go into detail
Compare	what are the similarities and differences?
Contrast	what are the differences?
Calculate	use numbers given to work out the value of something
Define	give the meaning of something
Evaluate	consider both sides - pros and cons
Justify	give evidence to explain something
To what extent	Judge the importance or success of something - has it worked or not
Argue	present a case with evidence or reasons
Assess	weigh up / give an informed judgement
Comment on	give your opinion on something

GCSE Foundation Level - Number | Day1

Formulas in the Exams

Use BODMAS when performing a calculation - Brackets, Others/Indices, Division, Multiplication, Addition, Subtraction

Decimals:

0.1 - this is $\frac{1}{10}$

0.01 - this is $\frac{1}{100}$

0.001 - this is $\frac{1}{1000}$

Factor: 1, 2, 3,4,6,12 are factors of 12.

Prime Factors: (Use Factor Tree and only contains prime numbers)

12 - prime factors are 2x2x3

HCF: 10 and 15 - 5 is the HCF.

Multiples: 6, 12, 18, 24 are multiples of 6.

LCM: 10, 15 - 30 is the LCM.

Checklist

Day #	Topics	Done	Notes
1	Number	☐	
2	Number	☐	
3	Algebra Basics	☐	
4	Graphs	☐	
5	Shapes	☐	
6	2D Shapes	☐	
7	3D Shapes	☐	
8	Algebra Intermediate	☐	
9	Ratio and Proportions	☐	
10	Percentages	☐	
11	Unit Conversions	☐	
12	Speed, Density, Pressure, Rates of Flow	☐	
13	Distance Time Graphs	☐	
14	Pythagoras' Theorem	☐	
15	Transformations	☐	
16	Projections	☐	
17	Angles	☐	
18	Probability	☐	
19	Loci	☐	
20	Bearings	☐	
21	Maps and Scale Drawings	☐	
22	Vectors	☐	
23	More Probabilities	☐	
24	Statistics	☐	
25	Statistics Continue	☐	
26	Trigonometry	☐	
27	Algebra Plus	☐	
28	Harder Graphs	☐	

Printed in Great Britain
by Amazon

25424129R00020